Unb

: A World War II Story of Survival, Resilience, and Redemption

by Laura Hillenbrand

: This is a quick read summary based on the book "Unbroken" by Laura Hillenbrand

Note to Readers:

This is a Summary & Analysis of "Unbroken" by Laura Hillenbrand. You are encouraged to buy the full version.

TABLE OF CONTENTS

INTRODUCTION

SUMMARY

In 1939, Louis Zamperini was training for his second Olympics, his eye on the once impossible 4 minute mile. His life stretched out before him, full of promise. Then the war began. The Olympics were cancelled. Pulled into conflict with the rest of the world, Louis enlisted in the Army Air Corps.

The Corps sent him to Hawaii as a bombardier on a B-24. When an air battle destroyed their plane and wounded most of their crew, Louis and the remaining men were transferred. Not long after, they were sent out on a rescue mission in a rickety plane that had been cannibalized for parts. The plane went down over the Pacific.

Adrift on a raft with his pilot and the new tail gunner, Louis floated for more than a month until their raft reached Japanese territory, where the living men were taken prisoner. He had already survived impossible odds, but the worst of his ordeal was only just cresting the horizon.

SETTINGS

The story begins in the small town of Torrance, California, where Louis was raised with his brother and two sisters, the children of Italian immigrants. It is the people who populate this setting that have the most effect on Louis, though there are certainly elements of small town life that play into Louis' behavior and theirs. It is in Torrance that Louis learns to steal, and to fight, and the bullies that torment him forge the beginnings of the strength he will need to survive World War II.

From Torrance, Louis moves on to Hawaii and the Pacific Theater. Though the war is unpleasant, it is at first little more than a distance thought, and Hawaii, where Louis is stationed, is a beautiful place. The soldiers there develop a camaraderie that compliments the landscape, spending their free time carousing with the girls at the officer's club and playing practical jokes. The barracks they live in aren't particularly nice, or particularly sturdy, but the company makes them a place Louis enjoys being, a stark contrast to barracks he will later live in. As the war moves closer, however, the setting begins to shift. The deaths of friends make the barracks seem strange, and on one of the islands where the crew stays between missions, Japanese bombs are dropped, turning the landscape strange and hostile. The imagery of cratered dirt and decapitated palm trees in place of lush jungle is a strong hint toward the troubles ahead.

The ocean is a common setting in survival stories. Its capricious and deadly nature lends itself well to a man vs nature struggle. For three men adrift on a rubber raft, it is a cruel setting. Things which had been pleasant – the sun, the sea itself – become enemies. But even in the hopeless drifting there are moments of beauty: a day when the sea is still and quiet, rain falling. Even the sharks have a kind of hard loveliness about them. This is due, in part, to Louis' attitude. He faces the sea as a challenge, and all that it can throw at him cannot take his mind even as it eats away at his body. This is an illustration of the way in which settings can be altered by the viewpoint character's feelings and thought process. Like the other places in which Louis had found himself, circumstances, and Louis' own state of mind, played a role in how they were seen and described for the reader.

The Japanese prison camps are nothing but bleak. They are hard, and cold, and there is nothing relieving about them. There are no moments of beauty. In such a setting, Louis finds himself wearing down, the dead landscape around him an extension of the hopelessness the men feel. With his own spirit slowly being ground down, Louis does not have the liberty to reimagine the setting that he did at sea or even in Torrance.

PLOT ANALYSIS

The story of Louis Zamperini's life is a long and winding one, and *Unbroken* is more survival story than sports biography, but it is that too. It has its bawdy moments, and its holy ones. By turns triumph and tragedy, and at times seemingly unbelievable, the account laid out in the pages of Lauren Hillenbrand's book takes the reader from California to Japan and back again, and to many place in between.

In his journeys, Louis faces not one antagonist, but many, and each of them has their own part to play in the plot. Beginning as something of a coming-of-age story, *Unbroken* first sets Louis most strongly against himself as he turns a life of theft and trouble into one of rigorous training and athletic excellence. When circumstances throw him into war, he faces other men, then nature. His experiences in Japan pit him against a country turned enemy, from which emerges a single reigning antagonist. Through it all, it is Louis' struggle to hold on to himself that carries the plot.

This struggle is not the driving force. The events which take Louis from start to finish also pull the reader along. Louis' struggle, however, is the heart of the story. It is what keeps the reader rooting for him, coming back to find out how he has held up under each new weight. Even at his worst, Louis is a sympathetic character, and the desire to see him have a happy ending is a strong motivator.

The plot itself is a bit unwieldly. It moves back and forth across countries, and jumps backwards and forwards in time. The constant motion can be somewhat confusing. It does, however, serve a purpose. Stories are complicated things, true stories especially, and in following the many, many threads of the account to their conclusions, Hillenbrand paints a deeply detailed picture of Louis' life.

HOW TO USE THIS GUIDE

This book is a companion to *Unbroken*, by Laura Hillenbrand, and does not contain the text of the book, so if you have not read it yet, you should get a copy before diving in. Some segments of the guide may contain spoilers.

The sections of this guide can be divided into two overarching categories: those that can be read along with the book, and those that should be explored after. The character and acronym guides may be useful for keeping track of those as you read, and the chapter by chapter analysis will offer a recap of events and some insight into them as you go along. The guide to settings is also handy to have around as you read.

Sections following the chapter analysis, from *Themes and Symbolism* to the final analysis should be read once you've finished the book. They contain spoilers, and commentary on sections of the book you'll want to have read first.

CHARACTERS

- *Louis Zamperini* – Olympic runner, WWII bombardier, captured by the Japanese

- *Anthony Zamperini* – Louis' father, a railroad electrician and Italian immigrant

- *Louise Zamperini* – Louis' mother, an Italian immigrant

- *Pete Zamperini* – Louis' older brother, a champion runner

- *Sylvia Zamperini* – Louis' younger sister

- *Virginia Zamperini* – Louis' younger sister

- *Glenn Cunningham* – Olympic miler, set the world record at 4:06.8 in 1934

- *Norman Bright* – American runner, set the two-mile world record in 1935

- *Don Lash* – A celebrated American runner Louis set his goals by

- *Frank Lubin* – American basketball player

- *Payton Jordan* – Louis' best friend, a sprinter at USC

- *Lauri Lehtinen* – Finnish runner, took the silver in the 5,000 at the 1936 Olympics
- *Gunnar Hockert* – Finnish runner, took gold in the 5,000 at the 1936 Olympics
- *Ilmari Salminen* – Finnish runner
- *Kunichi James "Jimmie" Sasaki* – a Japanese man Louis befriended at USC
- *Russell Allen Phillips* – the pilot of Louis' plane, called Phil by Louis
- *Cecile Perry* – Phil's fiancé back home
- *Stanley Pillsbury* – the plane engineer and top turret gunner
- *Clarence Douglas* – plane engineer and waist gunner
- *Robert Mitchell* – navigator and nose gunner
- *Frank Glassman* – radioman and belly gunner
- *Ray Lambert* – the tail gunner on *Super Man*
- *Harry Brooks* – radioman and waist gunner
- *George Moznette, Jr* – Copilot, not permanently attached to the crew

- *Charlton Hugh Cuppernell* – the copilot who replaced George Moznette

- *James Carringer* – Moznette's bombardier in his new crew

- *Major Johnathon Coxwell* – an American pilot, Phil's friend

- *Francis McNamara* – the tail gunner who replaced Lambert

- *Joe Deasy* – the pilot of *Daisy Mae*

- *George "Smitty" Smith* – an American pilot, a friend of Cecy's, acquainted with Phil

- *Kawamura* – a Japanese guard on Execution Island who befriends Louis and Phil

- *Suehara Kitamura* – the medical officer at Ofuna, known as the Quack

- *Commander Arthur Maher* – the ranking Allied POW at Ofuna, spoke Japanese

- *Commander John Fitzgerald* – the other ranking Allied POW at Ofuna, spoke Japanese

- *William Harris* – a friend of Louis' at Ofuna, spoke Japanese
- *Al Mead* – a POW at Omari who worked in the kitchens
- *Earnest Duva* – a POW at Omari who worked in the kitchens
- *Anton Minsass* – a prisoner at Ofuna
- *Fred Garrett* – a captured American pilot from a town near Louis', held at Ofuna
- *Frank Tinker* – a friend of Louis and Harris' at Ofuna
- *Reverend Phillips* – Allen Phillips' father
- *Kelsey Phillips* – Allen Phillips' mother
- *Mutsuhiro Watanabe* – a Japanese corporal at Omori, called The Bird
- *Yuichi Hatto* – the camp accountant at Omori
- *Tom Wade* – British POW, a barracks commander at Omari
- *Bob Martindale* – American POW, a barracks commander at Omari

- *Milton McMullen* – American POW at Omari, dedicated to sabotaging the Japanese
- *Kaname Sakaba* – the Japanese commander of Omari
- *Private Yukichi Kano* – camp interpreter at Omari who was kind to POWs
- *Lynn Moody* – a friend of Louis' who worked in the Office of War Information
- *Mansfield* – a POW at Omari
- *Prince Yoshimoto Tokugawa* – a Japanese dignitary
- *Lewis Bush* – a POW at Omari
- *Sergeant Oguri* – the Bird's replacement as Omari's commander
- *Hiroaki Kono* – a Japanese guard at Naoetsu
- *Ogawa* – a civilian guard
- *Alfred Weinstein* – a POW doctor at Mitsushima
- *Ken Marvin* – a marine, and a friend of Louis' at Naoetsu
- *Robert Trumbull* – an American journalist
- *Frank Rosynek* – a staff sergeant at Okinawa

- *Cynthia Applewhite* – a beautiful girl Louis falls in love with
- *Cynthia Zamperini* – Louis' daughter
- *Shizuka Watanabe* – the Bird's mother
- *Billy Graham* – an evangelist of rapidly growing fame
- *Draggen Mihailovitch* – a CBS reporter

MAIN CHARACTERS

Louis Zamperini:

In his youth, Louis Zamperini was a trouble maker. He stole from ncighbors and fought with bullies, refusing to cry when they beat him. As he grew older, he channeled his determination and will into running. His strong will was a tool that would serve him well in the war and the trials that came with it. For Louis, every obstacle was a challenge, and so he faced it, and pushed through where another man might have given up. It is this quality which has made his story so popular. People root for the underdog, and for the man who doesn't give up. Louis Zamperini was both.

Pete Zamperini:

Louis' older brother Pete was the golden boy. He was well-behaved, smooth talking, and liked by adults and children alike. The public perception of him, however, wasn't always accurate. His grades were low, and he was a companion in

Louis' pranks. Unlike Louis, he simply didn't get caught. Pete's love for his brother is a constant aspect of his character. It was he who trained Louis to run, taking him out every day, because he believed that Louis would be even better than he was in track. Pete, more than perhaps anyone except their mother, always believed in Louis.

Russell Allen Phillips:

Russell Allen Phillips, called Allen by his family and Phil by Louis, was Louis' pilot. He was a gentle man, who felt a deep responsibility for his men. Like Louis, he had an anchor in the struggles they faced. His deep faith in God and his devotion to his fiancé were the things that kept him going, even in the darkest times.

Francis McNamara:

The tail gunner who replaced Lambert, Francis McNamara was the third survivor of the *Green Hornet*'s crash, but the shock of it undid him. Where Louis had his own determination to see him through, and Phil had his faith, Mac struggled to find his footing in the long days at sea. He wore down quickly. His lack of hope, and its effect on him, makes him a perfect foil for the ever-determined Louis and the faithful Allen Phillips.

Mutsuhiro Watanabe:

By all accounts, Watanabe, known to his prisoners as the Bird, was a mad man and a sadist. He delighted in punishing POWs at the slightest excuse, and often without excuse at all. In his own mind, however, he was a good man pushed by the war. There were moments in which he seemed to want to project this, forcing POWs to play at being his friends, and seemingly believing that they were delighted to see him. As a primary antagonist, he looms larger than life, but he was still a human being, and this comes through in the story.

CHAPTER ANALYSIS

PREFACE

The story opens in 1943, on Louis Zamperini and two crewmates adrift on rotting rafts in the middle of the Pacific. In 27 days, they had drifted more than 1,000 miles. Hunger and dehydration had worn them to little more than bone, and the sun and the salt burned their skin. Sharks haunted the water around them. When a plane flew overhead, they waved it down, hoping for rescue, but the Japanese bomber strafed them with machine gun fire. Louis hid under the raft as the plane made a second pass, while his weakened companions lay unable to throw themselves into the water, and sharks circled below.

CHAPTERS 1-3

Louis Zamperini was born in 1917, to Italian immigrants. As a child he was active, always getting himself into trouble. As he grew, these tendencies only became more obvious. He stole food from the neighbors and played pranks constantly, then ran from retribution. The only thing that frightened him was a ride he was given in a plane.

Pete Zamperini, in contrast, was a well-spoken and well-liked young man who was very protective of his siblings. He was the role model Louis couldn't live up to, although his conduct was not as perfect as his reputation would imply. He was often right alongside Louis during his pranks.

Growing up, Louis was bullied for his looks and his race, but he never cried. He learned to defend himself, and became temperamental and violent. While his father tried physical punishment, his mother Louise, who shared Louis' love of mischief, kept tabs on him through his friends and tried stop trouble before it started.

As he reached his teens Louis had a moment of realization. He began to try and change, but his efforts went largely unnoticed, and he spent much of his time reading westerns and wishing to be somewhere else.

When he was fourteen, Pete began trying to get Louis into track, a sport in which Pete himself excelled. He trained him every day, despite Louis' protests. Louis improved, but in the summer of 1932 he ran away. He and the friend who went with him had a terrible experience, and when Louis came back he was much more amenable to training. Later that same summer, Louis stayed on the Cahuilla Indian Reservation for a time, and ran every day. When he returned home, he was completely dedicated to the sport.

He found a hero in the American miler Glenn Cunningham, and some popularity in school. After months of dedicated training, he went from barely making third to breaking local and state mile records for high school track. He won a two-mile race by a quarter mile. His star was officially on the rise.

In 1935, Louis broke the high school mile record, running the course in 4:21.3. Louis' athletic record redeemed his reputation in his hometown. He made it his goal to make the 1936 Olympics. Louis graduated high school. Because the Olympics had no mile race, milers ran the 1,500, but despite all his training Louis wasn't able to make the cut. He ran instead in the qualifying races for the 5,000 and made the final trial. The last race was in New York, where the record-setting temperatures ran the athletes down. Runners began dropping from the heat. Frontrunner Norman Bright's feet were burned so badly by the metal cleats in his shoes that he had to drop out of the race. Louis and the legendary Don Nash tied for first, and Louis became the youngest distance runner ever to make the Olympic team.

CHAPTERS 4-6

On the journey to Berlin, the tossing of the ship made training difficult, and Louis couldn't say no to the buffet. By the time they arrived in Germany at the end of July, he had gained 12 pounds.

The athletes were set up in the Olympic village, and on the 1st of August they attended the opening ceremony of the Olympics. The Germans had cleared all signs of conflict – and non-Aryans – from the streets. Louis didn't expect to win a medal. The Finnish runners were almost guaranteed to take the win.

In the qualifying heat, Louis came from behind and only took eighth, but he ran his final lap in less than a minute, beating the previous record of 69.2 by more than 13 seconds. After the race, he was introduced personally to Hitler, who remembered him as 'the boy with the fast finish.' On his way back to the village, Louis stole a German flag from the outside the Chancellery.

The Olympic team packed up and left on August 11th. With the eyes of the world turning elsewhere, Germany's anti-Semitism visibly resurfaced. Louis started attending the University of Southern California, and began training for the 1940 Olympics. Among his friends was a Japanese man called Jimmie.

Running with USC's track team, Louis continued breaking records. His idol Cunningham predicted that he would be the first to run a 4 minute mile, a feat previously deemed impossible. In 1938, Louis ran the NCAA Championship, hoping to meet that illustrious goal, but during the race he was assaulted by the other runners, who slashed his legs and punctured his foot with the spikes on their shoes, and an elbow to his side cracked a rib. Despite this, Louis took 1st, running the mile in 4:08.3, making his race the fastest NCAA mile in history.

In 1939, Louis won every race he ran, and he broke still more records in 1940. That same year, Hitler began the blitzkrieg and WWII started. The Olympics were canceled. Lost without the Olympics as a focus, Louis joined the Army Air Corps. The planes frightened him, so he washed out, going to work as an extra on a movie set, but he'd signed papers agreeing to return if called, and in November of 1941 he arrived in Texas to take up his post as a bombardier. Around the same time, Louis' friend Jimmie Sasaki was revealed to be a spy.

On December 7th, 1941, the Japanese attacked Pearl Harbor and America went to war. Louis was trained in bombsights and commissioned as a second lieutenant. Pete was a chief petty officer stationed with the Navy in San Diego. On August 19th, 1942, Louis left for his final stage of training in Ephrata, Washington, where he met his pilot, Allen Phillips, known to most as Phil, and the rest of the men assigned to crew No. 8 in the 372nd Bomb Squadron of the 307th Bomb Group, Seventh Air Force. Though Louis hoped to be assigned to a B-17 Flying Fortress, his crew was given a B-24 Liberator, a heavy, unwieldly plane plagued by mechanical trouble. They called it "the flying coffin."

The crew began their training. Louis' crew was one of the best in the squadron, and they worked together well. Phillips was especially praised for his skills as a pilot. Their plane had some mechanical quirks, but the men grew to think well of it.

In October 1942, Louis' crew was deployed, their training cut short to send them to Hawaii. They named their plane *Super Man*.

Louis' crew was posted in Oahu, on a base called Kahuku. They were not sent into combat, but continued training, where they had an accuracy rate in aerial gunning 3 times better than the squadron average, and Louis had excellent bomb scores. They also went out on ocean patrol, a duty that more often than not turned out to be incredibly boring. The men resorted to practical jokes to keep things interesting.

On the ground, Louis ran laps to keep up his training, and the men spent time in the North Shore officers club. Though there was fighting in Guadalcanal, the B-17s were sent into it while Louis' crew and their B-24 stayed in Oahu. This changed in December. On the 22nd, Louis and his crew were sent with 25 other planes to bomb the Japanese base on Wake Atoll.

Their mission was successful, but the 16 hour flight from Midway and back was pushing the fuel tanks to their limits, and on the return the bomb bay doors of *Super Man* were stuck open. They made the landing, barely, engines cutting out one after the other in their final approach. The last two died just as the plane reached its bunker. In the wake of the successful raid, America grew confident of its victory against Japan, and the men who had flown the bombers were hailed as heroes.

A training accident killed pilot George Moznette, who had temporarily been the copilot on *Super Man*, and his entire crew. These deaths, and others that had occurred in the short time Louis and his crew had been in Hawaii, unnerved them. In total, 35,933 American planes were lost in WWII, the majority of them in noncombat situations. The somewhat experimental nature of the new aircraft technology, along with the constant wear on the planes, factored heavily in their frequent crashes. Weather, and too-short runways, were also a problem. The B-24s were hard to maneuver, and the navigation equipment didn't always lead the pilots to their destinations. Add to that the dangers of combat, and the odds of death were very high.

In the Pacific, most planes in distress went down in the water. In a B-24, even if the pilot managed a safe landing, this was incredibly dangerous. The planes sank almost instantly, and getting to rafts was crucial, as sharks were known to take swift advantage of crash sites. Finding survivors was almost impossible in the vastness of the ocean, and rescuers often had very little idea where a plane had gone down. The rafts were small, and often went unseen even by pilots that passed directly over, and rescue planes went down as often as any other kind.

Men who did make it to the rafts were faced with provisions that quickly ran out, hunger, thirst, and exposure. Many died. Others went insane.

Worse than sharks and starvation, however, in the minds of the American airmen, was capture by the Japanese. They had all heard of the Rape of Nanking, in which more than 200,000 Chinese were tortured, raped, and murdered by Japanese soldiers.

The men were scared. They coped with it in different ways. Louis ran, listened to music, and took classes in survival and first aid. Phil, who felt responsible for his men, wrote letters to his fiancé, Cecy. All the men drank.

In April of 1943, Louis's crew was sent with 22 other bombers to attack Nauru, a phosphate-rich island taken by the Japanese. A lieutenant Donald Nelson flew with them, hoping to see combat. They received heavy return fire, and were attacked by Zeros as they turned toward home. *Super Man* took massive damage under the rain of machine gun fire.

Ray Lambert, the tail gunner, took shrapnel in his left leg. At the waist guns, Clarence Douglas and Harry Brooks too were hit by shrapnel, and in the bottom turret Frank Glassman was hit in the back. Nelson was shot in the stomach. In the top turret, gunner Stanley Pillsbury's leg was pierced with the remains of the turret wall.

Louis, sent by Phil, went out and pulled the wounded Brooks back to the flight deck, where he passed out. He closed the bomb bay doors, which had opened when the hydraulic lines were fractured, taking out their landing gear and brakes.

Seeing the other shot men, Louis called for help, and Charlton Cuppernell, the copilot, ran back to aid him while Phil struggled to keep control of the plane. Cuppernell and Louis tried to patch up the men, and Louis realized Pillsbury was wounded too when he felt blood dripping down on his shoulder from the top turret. As Louis attempted to help him, one of the Zeros swung back for another round, and Pillsbury shot it out of the sky. Douglas took out the third with the waist gun.

With the immediate danger over, Louis laid Pillsbury out next to Brooks, tended to him, and went to assess the plane. The right rudder was destroyed. The cables which gave the pilot control were damaged. Phil had to hold the yolk down with his feet to keep the plane from tipping upward and onto its back. Funafuti, their landing site, was a five hour flight, and they would have to make the landing without brakes on a runway already too short for a B-24.

As they neared Funafuti, the men cranked the landing gear down, and Louis tied each of the injured men to something stable, but didn't knot the cords in case the plane caught fire. Despite a flat left tire, they made the landing without further mishap. The ground crew would later count 594 holes in *Super Man*. Harry Brooks died in the infirmary.

CHAPTERS 10-12

The night after the American raid on Nauru, the Japanese retaliated. There were no bomb shelters, and the men scrambled for cover; Phil and Louis spent the night hiding under a native's hut. The B-24s, lined up for a mission, were hit with two bombs. Funafuti was left in shambles.

Louis and Phil were sent back to Hawaii with Cuppernell, the navigator Robert Mitchell, and Glassman. Douglas was too injured to fight any longer, and Lambert would be months healing. Pillsbury's leg was destroyed. It was the end of *Super Man* and the original crew.

Restless and unassigned, Phil and Louis spent much of their time drinking until they and the other men from *Super Man* were transferred to the 42nd squadron of the 11th Bomber Group, stationed at Kualoa. The missing crew were replaced by six new men, and they awaited a plane.

On May 27th, 1943, Louis and Phil were sent out to look for a missing B-24. They were given *Green Hornet*, a plane that barely managed to stay in the air, its already tenuous existence made even more so by crewman scavenging it for parts. They set off with ten crew and one passenger, alongside the B-24 *Daisy Mae*, to search for the missing plane.

Green Hornet, flying with its tail below its nose, couldn't keep up with *Daisy Mae,* and Phil radioed the pilot to go on ahead. In the afternoon, shortly after *Green Hornet* reached the search area, engine one failed. The engineer, called to the cockpit to stop engine one's propellers, mistakenly stopped engine two. *Green Hornet* spiraled. The men prepared to crash.

The plane blew apart on contact. Louis, trapped in trailing wires, tried to fight his way to the surface. Phil escaped the cockpit with a head injury. Free of the wires, Louis found his way out of the fuselage and floated to the surface in his life vest, nearly drowned. The only other survivor was their new tail gunner, Francis "Mac" McNamara. Louis swam for one of the drifting life rafts, rowed to the second, and took them back to the others. Phil, woozy with the wound to his head, put Louis in command.

Their only provisions were those in the rafts, consisting of several military issue chocolate bars, and a few tins of water. There were a few tools aboard, and patch kits for the rafts, but nothing else. Louis assigned two squares of chocolate a day to each man, and two or three sips of water. Mac was uninjured, but in addition to his head wound Phil had a broken finger, and Louis's ribs had broken against the gun mount when the plane hit water. Sharks circled the rafts, and night fell.

CHAPTERS 13-15

Daisy Mae returned to base without *Green Hornet*, and 4:30am on May 28th, Phil and Louis' crew was declared missing. In the rafts, Louis woke to find that Mac had eaten all of the chocolate. Determined that they would be rescued, and knowing that Mac was unmoored by the shock of the crash, he took it calmly.

In the afternoon, a B-25 flew overhead. Louis shot a flare and shook out a dye pack into the water around them. The plane didn't turn. Its direction told Louis that they were drifting west, away from American flight paths.

On May 30th, a B-24 search plane flew overhead. Again Louis shot off flares, but they went unseen, and *Daisy Mae* flew on.

The fifth day, Mac screamed that they were going to die until Louis slapped him to shut him up. They ran out of water.

After a week, the search for survivors from *Green Hornet* was ended. The men's belongings were sent home, and telegrams sent to their families informing them that they were missing. Newspapers and radios ran stories on the missing Olympic miler. Louis' mother Louise refused to believe that he was dead.

Louis, Phil, and Mac floated, ravaged by sun and salt, using torn open air pump cases to catch water. They had fishing line and hooks, but no bait. After nine days, Louis caught and killed an albatross that had landed on their still bodies. It smelled too foul to eat, but they used the meat as bait. Louis feared they would go insane, and tried to keep their minds clear with trivia. The men recited the preparation of meals to each other in place of food. Phil and Louis talked about their plans for the future. Mac, deeply depressed, hardly spoke.

The rafts began to decompose. The men caught a second albatross and ate it. Occasionally they caught fish or birds. Phil's head wound healed. They passed 21 days at sea. Each time water ran out they prayed for more rain.

After 27 days, another plane flew over, returning when the men signaled. It strafed the rafts with machine gun fire. The first time, they jumped into the water. The second, only Louis had the strength. He tied himself to the raft with a cord to keep from being swept away by the current. A shark attacked. Louis hit it in the nose, and then again. The bullets stopped, and Louis pulled himself back onto the raft.

The Japanese plane returned four times. Each time, Louis jumped into the water and fought off sharks. Neither Mac nor Phil was hit. The plane dropped a depth charge, but it didn't go off. The second raft was cut in half, and all three men had to share the remaining one.

Their raft, leaking air, began to sink. Sharks tried to drag the men over the edges, and they fought them off with oars. They hooked up the air pump, and pumped fast enough to keep the raft from sinking completely. Louis began patching. The battle with the sharks, and the struggle to keep the raft afloat, went on for hours.

Louis pulled apart the ruined raft and used the canvas to make a sun shade. He and Phil talked over the encounter with the Japanese, and realized that they must be very far west, with some 850 miles between them and land, which they calculated they would reach on day 46 or 47.

CHAPTERS 16-18

A pair of sharks attacked the raft, and Louis was surprised to be saved by Mac, who helped him beat them off with the oars. Deciding to return the attack, Louis caught a small shark with his hands around its tail, and they ate the liver. They caught a second, but no more. Mac grew ever more lifeless.

Around the thirtieth day, the men were woken from sleep by a great white shark attack, but the creature gave up after playing with the raft for a while. They caught another albatross, and gave the blood to Mac, who couldn't sit up. He grew weaker as the days passed, and Louis shared water with him. On their 33rd day, Mac died.

Phil and Louis continued to drift west, growing thinner and weaker. They began to see birds, and planes. On their 46th day, July 14th, as a storm began that lifted the raft on swelling waves, they saw an island.

As one island became a chain ahead, Phil and Louis rowed alongside them, waiting for the cover of night, and the storm became a typhoon. Louis tied them into the raft to keep the waves from throwing them overboard. The storm calmed, and set them down between two islands. As they rowed toward shore, a boat caught sight of them.

The sailors aboard the ship took them prisoner, and they were taken to an infirmary to be treated for starvation and exposure, where they discovered that in the 46 days of their journey they had drifted 2,000 miles, and landed in the Marshall Islands. Both had lost more than half their body weight.

After 2 days, Louis and Phil were transferred to Kwajelin, the place known as "Execution Island." They reached it on July 16th, and were blindfolded and carried, locked in separate wooden cells with dirt floors. They were given little food and less water, and Louis was severely ill. The guards tormented them, beating and harassing them, forcing them at gunpoint to sing and dance.

When Louis had been on Kwajelin for a week, he was taken to be interrogated. Knowing they had captured a B-24D, Louis told the truth about the plane, but lied and feigned ignorance about aspects of the new B-24E. He practiced lying in his cell so he could fool them if they asked him again. A new guard, called Kawamura, befriended Louis and Phil, and his small kindnesses made an enormous difference in their outlooks.

Three weeks into their time on Kwajelin, Louis and Phil were injected with an experimental substance that made them sick. A short while later, both contracted dengue fever. Louis was taken to be interrogated again, and pretended to give in, telling the Japanese the location and number of fake bases in Hawaii.

On August 24th, the Japanese decided to send Louis and Phil to a POW camp in Yokohama, Japan. Two days later, they were led out to a Japanese ship. They had been on Kwajelin for 6 weeks.

CHAPTERS 19-21

The trip took 3 weeks. At its end, Louis was given a bath and his head and beard shaved, and then he was led into a room where he met Jimmie Sasaki, the Japanese man he had befriended at USC. Sasaki had been made head interrogator of all POWs in Japan. After some awkward conversation, Louis was taken out in the POW compound.

Louis discovered that he was not in a POW camp, but a secret interrogation facility called Ofuna. He was told he would not be allowed to speak to any of the other prisoners, or make eye contact. He would have to ask for water and to use the bathroom. Every infraction was punished with beatings.

At Ofuna, the men each had their own cell in the flimsy barracks, and every morning at 6am they were woken for roll call. They were given breakfast, then forced to clean the barracks floor. When that was done, they were sent outside and made to exercise, then left to sit out on the benches. The men were beaten frequently. What little food was given was often spoiled and contaminated. Illness ran rampant.

The guards at Ofuna were men who hadn't made it in the Japanese military, and many were sadists. This, combined with the racism instilled in them, and a cultural belief that to be captured was the ultimate shame, made for a dangerous mix. The few who tried to treat captives humanely were attacked by their own peers.

Rescue, while hoped for, was unlikely. The Japanese had orders to kill all POWs if Allied forces came near reaching them.

Prisoners at Ofuna communicated in whispers and hand signals. Louis occasionally saw Phil, who once told him that he felt responsible for the deaths of their crew, and that he would never fly again. He also saw Sasaki, who wanted to chat with him like friends, and seemed to be protecting Louis from the worst of interrogation at the camp.

Because the guards could not speak English, prisoners sometimes spoke with each other by pretending to talk to the guards. They also wrote notes on toilet paper and hid them for others in the bathroom. They used Morse code. Even that small defiance helped keep their spirits up. Louis kept a secret diary in a little handmade book that was given to him by another prisoner. The men were eager for any news of the war, brought with new prisoners. When they could, they stole newspapers. Louis' friend William Harris kept an address book and a Japanese-English dictionary he was writing, as well as hand drawn maps of the war zones, all hidden from the guards.

Winter came, and more prisoners fell ill. The Japanese stole the rations sent to feed the prisoners, and in place of food the men took up smoking. When a Japanese news editor came to the camp with a folder of information on Louis, the men set him up against a Japanese running in a race he lost badly. Louis went to Sasaki to try and get better treatment for the men, but despite talking as though he would help he did nothing, and Louis began to believe that Sasaki wasn't protecting him after all, that he hadn't been interrogated because the Japanese weren't interested in what he knew. Two prisoners who worked in the kitchen snuck extra food to Louis on the condition that he share it with Phil; after their long days adrift at sea, the two of them were the most malnourished men in the camp.

The rules changed at the end of 1943, and prisoners were allowed to speak to each other, though new transfers were kept in solitary until they were interrogated.

Extra food, as well as a coat given to him by another prisoner, and friendship with Harris and a prisoner called Frank Tinker helped Louis through the winter. In the spring, he was made to race against another Japanese runner. This time, Louis, light from starvation and helped by the extra calories, won. He was beaten for it. They brought in a third runner, who bribed Louis with a rice ball to throw the race so the runner could win in front of his girlfriend. Later in the spring, Phil was taken from Ofuna, allegedly to be sent to a POW camp called Zentsuji, where he would be registered with the Red Cross and allowed to write home. He was instead sent to Ashio, where POWs were forced to mine copper. Phil was told he would be allowed to write home, but later found his letter on the garbage heap, partly burned.

Back home, the Zamperinis believed that Louis still lived. When he had been missing for a month, his mother wrote a letter to the commander of the Seventh Air Force asking him not to give up the search. He wrote back to say that nothing had been found and the family should accept this. Pete, training Navy recruits in San Diego, grew thin and worried. Sylvia, whose husband was away on the front, moved back in with her parents and her sister Virginia. In October of 1943, Louis' possessions arrived back home. His mother, who had developed a rash on her hands when she heard of him missing, refused to open the trunk, and had it sent down to the basement. Sylvia wrote letters to her husband and to Louis.

In January 1944, the Americans captured Kwajelin, where they found the name Louis Zamperini etched on a shard of the wreckage. Papers found on the island were taken to Joe Deasy, the pilot of *Daisy Mae*, who read the descriptions of two American airmen held there and was sure they were Louis and Phil. The families were not notified.

Like the Zamperinis, the Phillips family did not believe their son was dead. His fiancé Cecy, in particular, held to the belief that he must be alive. The families of *Green Hornet*'s crew began corresponding. In June of 1944, the war department declared all the men aboard *Green Hornet* dead. Both the Phillips family and the Zamperinis refused to believe it.

CHAPTERS 22-24

While they were walking together in the summer of 1944, Louis heard planes, and asked Tinker if he would be able to fly one, if they could escape the camp. Tinker assured Louis he could, and they began a plot to escape with Harris.

Louis, starving, got a job working as a barber for the guards, and was paid with a rice ball for every customer. As the war news grew worse for the Japanese, the captives had cause to fear a kill-all order, and were told that if Japan lost the war they would all be executed. In July, Louis stole a paper that proved the Allies were closing in. A new captive confirmed that Saipan had fallen. They began to hear air-raid sirens in the distance. The guards stole more of the food, and the beatings grew worse.

When they were given an almanac by a guard, Louis and Harris poured over it, deciding to escape by boat, walking across Japan to reach a port on the western side from which they could reach China. They walked in the yard to strengthen their legs, and stoles supplies. The plan was suspended when a prisoner escaped from a POW camp, and orders came down that for every any escape would be answered by the execution of captive Allied officers.

In September, Louis was sent in to steal a newspaper from the desk of Ofuna's medical officer, a particularly cruel guard the men called the Quack. He snuck in while the guards were on a smoke break, showed it to Harris, who had a photographic memory, then returned it to the office before it was reported missing.

Shortly after, the Quack caught Harris with a drawing of the map. Searching his cell, he found more maps, as well as stolen newspaper clippings, and the Japanese-English dictionary Harris had been working on, which contained military terms. That night, the Quack called all the captives out to the yard, forced them to do pushups and hold a stress position, then beat Harris in front of them for nearly an hour. Harris was so badly injured that he couldn't remember his friends' names.

On September 30th, 1944 Louis, along with Tinker and several other prisoners, was sent to a POW camp called Omori. The camp stood in Tokyo bay, on a sandy, man-made island. On their first day there, they met Corporal Mutsuhiro Watanabe, called The Bird by the prisoners. He hit Louis for dropping his eyes, demanding to know why Louis wouldn't look at him. When Louis did, The Bird hit him again. Later, when they were led to a cold outdoor quarantine area and left for hours, Louis started a fire with a spindle and piece of an apple box. The Bird beat him for it.

Watanabe, who grew up wealthy, had expected to be an officer when he joined the army. He was instead assigned as a corporal, and when he was assigned to Omori, he took out his anger at the denial on the prisoners. At Omori, as in other Japanese POW camps, enlisted prisoners were treated like slaves. Officers, who weren't forced to work, were given half rations. Watanabe kept prisoners in a state of terror, beating them for nothing and torturing them psychologically and emotionally. He constantly changed rules and beat prisoners for breaking them. Sometimes, he apologized. He forced prisoners to be his friends, then treated them more harshly than before. Watanabe particularly hated officers. Most particularly, he hated Louis Zamperini.

After quarantine, Louis was moved into the barracks, where he was introduced to barracks commanders Tom Wade and Bob Martindale. Louis was warned that the Bird would beat anyone he heard talking about him, and to never use his name, and that he liked to send the guards into the barracks to demand that the prisoners salute, then come through the door or a window and beat someone. He also ordered that prisoners salute his office window. Those Omari was a POW camp, prisoners were not allowed to write letters home, and though other prisoners were registered with the Red Cross, Louis was not.

Every day, the Bird hunted Louis down and beat him for invented transgressions. Louis refused to be cowed. He ordered that the officers would be made to work, a violation of international law, and beat anyone who disagreed until Louis suggested making them work in the camp. Watanabe ordered them to sew leather packs for the military, and empty the latrines. The men, officers and enlisted both, did everything they could to see that supplies for the military were made badly, sent to the wrong addresses, and broken whenever possible. They also stole. They had systems for hiding the stolen goods during inspections, and practiced thieves trained others to steal. Men stopped dying from malnutrition, and thriving black market grew up in the camp.

On October 18th, 1944, a Japanese show called *Postman Calls*, which aired in English for Allied troops, sent a message from Louis Zamperini to his family, stating that he was alive and well. Louis knew nothing about the message. The show was not broadcast in the United States, but the news was picked up by a man working for a group that informed the families of POWs about their whereabouts. He misunderstood the name, sending the information to the wrong address, and it was not mailed on to Torrance until January of 1945.

CHAPTER 25-28

On November 1st, 1944, Louis caught his first glimpse of B-29 Superfortress as it flew over Tokyo. The enormous planes had been designed after his capture, and one could fly from Saipan to Tokyo and back, a feat no other plane could accomplish. For the men in Omari, it was a beacon of hope. For the Japanese, it was a warning, and it inspired the Bird's cruelty to new heights. He beat Louis across the head with the buckle of his belt, making him temporarily deaf in his left ear.

Later in November, Louis was approached by men from Radio Tokyo, who had a transcript of his death announcement and asked him to come on *Postman Calls* and announce that he was alive. At first reluctant, Louis accepted the offer. He was careful to write a message that spoke well of the Japanese so it would be sure to go through.

The program first aired a teaser episode, sharing that Louis was alive. In California, Lynn Moody, a friend of Louis', was working in the Office of War Information, typing transcripts for propaganda analysts. She was ecstatic to hear the message. Two days later, on November 20th, Louis' personal message was aired. It was intercepted, and played on several American stations, and people all over the country sent messages to the Zamperinis about its existence. Careful details Louis had put into the message convinced his family of its truth.

Radio Tokyo invited Louis back for another broadcast. This time, they gave him a message they'd written, decrying the US War Department for lying about the whereabouts of their soldiers. The Japanese had kept him alive, it seemed, to make him read propaganda, waiting until he was declared dead so they could call the American government unreliable. Louis refused to read the message. The producers promised him a comfortable room of his own and freedom from the POW camp. Louis refused again, and was sent back to Omari and daily beatings that only grew worse.

On November 24th, a fleet of B-29 bombers flew over Tokyo and dropped their load. Sightings of the planes were daily after that, and with each one the Bird grew more anxious, and more vicious.

Phil had been transferred to Zentsuji. The men were so starved they had to eat weeds, and their only water was filthy runoff from rice patties. They were, however, registered with the Red Cross, and in December his family was informed that he was alive. His fiancé quit her job and moved to Indiana to wait for him to come home.

After Christmas, the beatings from the Bird abruptly stopped. An important dignitary, Prince Yoshimoto Tokugawa, had been informed by a POW named Lewis Bush of the way the Bird behaved. The prince informed the Red Cross and the War Office, and asked that something be done. At the end of December, the Bird was sent away from Omari. Though he was promoted to sergeant and sent to another camp, Louis, at least, was safe from his attentions.

The camp interpreter, Private Kano, who had always been kind to the POWs, worked with Sergeant Oguri, who replaced the Bird, and saw that the men were treated better and allowed to write home. Prisoners transferred from Ofuna arrived, among them Bill Harris, who had been beaten again by the Quack and was in a constant state of confusion. A POW doctor declared him near death. When the Red Cross relief boxes were finally handed out, Louis gave his to Harris, and he seemed to improve. Despite the new leadership, however, American victories and the constant bombing runs by the B-29s made the guards anxious and harsh, and the prisoners feared a kill-all order. This fear was made deeper by news from Palawan of 150 prisoners burned alive in fear of an American landing on the island.

February 16th and 17th, an air battle was fought over Tokyo, and the Japanese lost 500 planes, as well as the airport. Less than two weeks later, Louis, along with his Tom Wade, Frank Tinker, the kitchen worker Al Mead who had snuck him food, and Commander John Fitzgerald – who had been with Louis at Ofuna – was transferred to Naoetsu, a prison camp on the western shore of Japan. The winter was freezing, and the snow was 14 feet deep. To Louis' shocked horror, it was also the camp to which the Bird had been transferred.

The guards stole the Red Cross relief boxes, and the prisoners, most of whom were Australian, starved. Louis grew ill in the cold. The Bird beat him frequently. At Naoetsu, the enlisted POWs worked long, dangerous shifts in the factories, and in the spring the Bird ordered the officers to be sent out as farm laborers, in defiance of the Geneva Convention. Fitzgerald, who had the position of senior POW, thought it was a good way to get the men out from under the Bird's nose every day.

In April, the first B-29 the men had seen since Tokyo flew overhead. The men were excited; the Bird was furious. When the civilian guard made a joke about the officers' work ethic, the Bird sent them to load coal on the barges as punishment. They stole available food to keep their spirits up. Sometimes, hauling salt, they stole that too.

One day, while carrying a heavy basket of salt on his back, Louis was tripped by a guard and fell, badly injuring his leg. Because he couldn't work, his rations were halved. For a while he tailored the guard's uniforms in exchange for rations, but when that failed he had to go to the Bird and plead for a job. The Bird ordered him to clean the sty of a pig kept on the compound, and told him he would have to do it without tools. Louis, who had always been a very clean person, was forced to pick up pig excrement with his hands, and ate scraps of the pig's food to keep from starving to death.

CHAPTERS 29-31

Bombs were dropped on Naoetsu in May. A little more than a week later, 400 new POWs were transferred to the camp. The new men had news: many of Japan's larger cities had been bombed, and Germany had been defeated.

In June, Louis was healed enough to go back to work. Some of the men in his work party stole fish, and the Bird singled out the thieves and several officers – Louis, Tinker, and Wade among them – and ordered each of the enlisted men in the work party to punch them in the face.

B-29s flew overhead every day, and rations grew scarce. Seeing starving civilians as sick as they were, the POWs stopped stealing food from their work sites. The Americans grew closer, and the POWs were told the kill-all order would be coming soon. At Zentsuji, Phil and the other Americans were separated from the rest and driven out to a remote place where they were forced to hike up a mountain in the dark and the rain to a camp called Rokuroshi. The prisoners at Naoetsu were told that they would be executed in August.

Coal hauling was stopped, and Louis again went to the Bird to beg for work. He was given a sick goat and ordered to keep it alive on pain of his own death. Though Louis nursed it carefully, the goat was untied one night and stuffed itself on grain. It died. The Bird ordered Louis out into the yard and forced him to lift a heavy wooden beam. Louis, determined not to let the Bird break him, held it over his head for 37 minutes, until the Bird attacked him and forced him to drop it.

On August 1st, the US sent 836 B-29s to drop bombs on Nagaoka, a path that took them over Naoetsu. Nagaoka burned. Elsewhere, planes dropped leaflets warning citizens to evacuate before heavy bombing began.

Louis grew sicker with the dysentery that had plagued him for much of his time in the camps. The Bird's torments continued to grow worse. He threatened to drown Louis, then beat him instead, promising a drowning later. Louis, pushed beyond his limits, met with the other officers and plotted to kill the Bird.

They planned to drag him up to the top floor of the barracks, tie him to a rock, and throw him down into the river below.

On August 6th, the Americans dropped an atomic bomb on Hiroshima. August 9th, Nagasaki was hit. Six days later, news of Japan's surrender came to Naoetsu. Work was stopped, but the guards weren't telling the prisoners why. Louis was ill with both dysentery and beriberi. It was not until August 20th that the guards would officially announce the end of the war to the POWs at Naoetsu. As the men bathed in the river – an unprecedented luxury – an American plane flew over, signaling a confirmation: the war was ended. The plane also had gifts for the POWs – chocolate, cigarettes, and a magazine with an article about the atomic bomb.

CHAPTERS 32-34

Phil, in Rokuroshi, knew very little of what was going on in the outside world. On August 22nd, the commander of the camp returned from a disappearance, declared the war ended, and gave his sword over to the ranking POW. All the guards left. The men built a bonfire and threw a party.

At Naoetsu, American planes flew over and dropped food, but not enough. Fitzgerald had the men write "700 POWs here." A few days later, 6 B-29s flew over and dropped enough food for an army.

On September 2nd, Japan's official surrender ended World War II.

B-29s continued to drop food, clothes, and medical supplies to the POWs, who shared them with starving and ill villagers and even with the guards. The men were told that an evacuation team would arrive on September 4th. They spent their time eating and exploring the countryside.

When September 4th passed without news, the men took matters into their own hands and demanded a train. The next day, they marched out of the camp and boarded, headed for Yokohama and then home. All over the country, other trains carried POWs toward home.

Louis was sent to Okinawa, where he discovered that many of his friends were dead or gone home. Because he wasn't ever registered with the Red Cross, he was at first not allowed access to the mess or given a new uniform. When a reporter asked about his running career, Louis told him it was over.

September 9th, the headline "Zamperini Comes Back from Dead" ran in the *Los Angeles Times*. His family was thrilled.

In remote Rokuroshi, the B-29s did not come with provisions until September 2nd, and it was not until a week later that Phil and the other men were retrieved from the camp and taken to Yokohama. On September 16th, his family was officially informed of his liberation.

Louis stayed in Okinawa for more than a week before he went on to Hawaii, where he was put in a hospital with Fred Garrett, who had been with him at Ofuma. He had been promoted to captain.

On October 16th, Phil made it home to Indiana. A month later, he married Cecy. Louis ended up in a hospital in San Francisco, where Pete met him, seeing his brother again for the first time in years. The army sent a plane that picked them both up, and Louis at last went home. At first, he seemed fine, but cracks in his composure soon began to appear.

As the stories of former POWs were taken, among the names of the worst abusers was Mutsuhiro Watanabe, the Bird. Watanabe had disappeared before the liberation of Naoetsu, but the police were determined to hunt him down.

Louis was once again a celebrity, and people lined up to hear his story. Though he kept up a pleasant façade, Louis struggled with anxiety and suffered from nightmares. He began drinking. In Miami Beach he met Cynthia Applewhite, and the two began dating. After less than two weeks, they were engaged. They planned a wedding for June, just three months away.

To impress Cynthia, Louis gave up drinking and smoking. He resigned from active duty, becoming a captain in the Air Force Reserve. The first Olympic Games since 1936 were announced for July 1948 in London, two years away. Louis began training to run once more.

In May, Cythia's disapproving parents gave her permission to visit Louis if they waited to be married until the fall. Louis introduced her to his family, but fearing he was losing her, suggested calling off the engagement. Instead, they set a date for the 25th of May, and married in a simple ceremony at the church Cynthia had attended as a child.

CHAPTERS 35-37

Though they tried to put on brave faces, Louis, as well as Phil and other men released from the POW camps, were struggling. Beyond the physical effects, many of them permanent, most of the men suffered from PTSD and a large number had anxiety disorders.

Louis struggled to find a job that would buy him and Cynthia a house of their own. They managed an apartment. Their honeymoon had been peaceful, but after it Louis' nightmares returned. He kept running, training for 1948, but it exacerbated his war injury, and ruined his leg. His nightmares redoubled. He started drinking and smoking again, and suffered from flashbacks. He decided on a goal: kill the Bird.

Watanabe was hiding in a mountain province of Japan, passing as a laborer while the hunt for war criminals went on. Jimmie Sasaki, it turned out, had not been chief interrogator at Ofuna, but an interpreter. He was sentenced to 6 years of hard labor for war crimes. In the fall of 1946, the Bird was found dead in the mountains with a woman who was most likely his lover.

Back home, Louis didn't hear any news of the Bird's death. He spent his time training with a punching bag, and trying to raise money to get to Japan. Two years passed. Louis' business ventures kept failing. His drinking grew worse. Cynthia was frightened, and then angry. They began fighting, often physically. In 1948, Cynthia got pregnant. Later that year, while dreaming about strangling the Bird, Louis wrapped his hands around his wife's throat in his sleep.

Cynthia Zamperini was born in the first month of 1949. Louis loved her, but his alcohol addiction was only getting worse, and his wife left him to go home to her parents.

CHAPTERS 38-EPILOGUE

Officials began to question the Bird's death. Details came up that didn't make sense. His mother was certain he was alive. In 1946 they began watching his family again. On October 1st, 1948, Watanabe met his mother at a restaurant in Tokyo. Their meeting was brief. They planned another for 2 years later.

Billy Graham came to Los Angeles in the fall of 1949. Cynthia had come back to live with Louis until the divorce went through. In October, Cynthia went to one of his meetings. Convincing Louis to return with her took days; the sermon left Louis uncertain and afraid. Once more, Cynthia convinced him to go. Listening to Graham speak of miracles, Louis remembered Mac and Phil surviving the strafing by the Japanese plane, the beauty of a moment when the sea had gone still around them. When Graham called for prayer, he stood up to leave, but he remembered, suddenly, a promise he had made, praying on the raft, to serve God if He saved them.

He turned and walked up to the front. That night when they got home, he dumped out his liquor and threw away his cigarettes. The next morning he went out to the park with his bible and read.

Louis started speaking around the country about his story, and he and Cynthia were finally able to afford a house, though they still struggled with money. In 1950, Louis went back to Japan, and visited Sugamo Prison, where the guards of the POW camps were being held. Only the Bird was not there. His mother, whom he had promised to meet that year, had not seen him, and believed he was dead. The guard at Sugamo told Louis that they believed the Bird had committed suicide. Louis was surprised to feel compassion. He shook the hands of each of the men who had been guards at the camps where he was held, and felt at last that the war was over.

In 1954, Louis began the Victory Boys Camp, taking in troubled boys and sharing the mountains and his own story with them. He continued speaking around the country, and received numerous awards and dedications. He was asked to carry the torch for five Olympic Games. Along with their daughter, Cynthia and Louis had a son, Luke, and Louis remained physically active even as he reached his nineties and beyond.

Phil, who went by his middle name Allen at home, became a teacher and had 2 children with Cecy. He died in 1998. Pete Zamperini married and had 3 children; he coached track and football, and shared his brother's legacy with anyone who asked. He died of cancer in 2008.

In 1996, Louis discovered that the Bird was alive. He had reappeared in 1952, after the arrest order for war criminals had been suspended following the 1950 treaty that ended the occupation of Japan because the US needed them as allies in the Cold War. The treaty took effect in 1952, and the war criminals were reprieved. Every Japanese war criminal who hadn't already been executed was freed by 1958 and all were granted amnesty.

Watanabe married and had 2 children, and ran a profitable insurance company in Tokyo. Most people still thought he was dead until 1995, when he spoke to a *Daily Mail* reporter and apologized for his actions.

Upon learning that the Bird was alive, Louis asked to see him. In 1997, a CBS reporter sat down with Watanabe for an interview about his treatment of the POWs, most particularly Louis Zamperini. Watanabe deflected, but agreed to meet with Louis and personally apologize for his actions. When Louis came to Japan, however, Watanabe changed his mind. Louis never did get to speak to him.

In 1998, Louis ran through the village of Naoetsu with the Olympic torch, cleansing his memories of the place.

THEMES AND SYMBOLS

Dignity:

Dignity comes up frequently in *Unbroken*. Again and again it is referenced as essential to human life, and the evidence would seem to support the claim. In the camps, the Japanese defied the Geneva Convention, and men were treated like animals. The POWs went to almost any length to reclaim some part of their defiance – some part of their dignity – stealing, sabotaging, and wreaking havoc as often as they could get away with it.

These actions, theft especially, may seem a strange way to reclaim lost dignity, when theft is often considered to be such a dishonest and dishonorable action, the lazy man's means of getting by. For the Japanese POWs, however, theft – especially of food – was a necessity. More than that, it was a way of getting a little bit of their own back from captors who had no respect for them.

Courage:

What Louis and Phil and many others suffered at the hands of the Japanese, it takes more than a strong constitution to survive. It takes courage: the courage to keep going when the best that can be hoped for is the next day being only as miserable as the last, and the courage to face violence and hatred with poise.

Every day at Omari, Louis was beaten by the Bird, and each day he looked back with defiance in his eyes. When Radio Tokyo offered him a position as a propaganda prisoner with a comfortable bed and no more beatings, he chose to go back to the Bird's vicious treatment at Omari rather than betray his country even in a small fashion. Commander Fitzgerald, one of the ranking officers at Ofuna and later at Omari and Naoetsu, was tortured viciously for information, and refused to give in. Countless others sharing their prisons did the same.

Human Cruelty:

That very fact that stories such as Louis Zamperini's exist is a testament to the capacity humans have for cruelty, and for destruction. In an era when the entire world was at war, this point was driven home again and again. In Japan, where citizens who protested the prison camps could be called enemies of the state, and guards caught being kind to POWs were beaten by their fellows, prisoners from other nations saw it up close and personal. But it was not only those on the Axis side of the war who taught hatred and racism to their people. Nationalism, and with it loathing for any who were not allies – and even some who were – was a frequent refrain in every country involved.

REAL WORLD TRUTH

Though the title of the book is *Unbroken*, Louis, and the many other POWs who made it back to their own countries, did not return home unscathed. Before his conversion and subsequent change, Louis was an alcoholic. He suffered flashbacks and severe anxiety, both symptoms of a condition now known as Post Traumatic Stress Disorder. As the book notes, more than a quarter of Pacific POWs struggled with the condition, and with other associated mental illnesses. Many hoarded food after the long starvation of the camps. Others suffered from nightmares and even hallucinations. Alcoholism was a common response.

Men who had not served as POWs were not immune to these conditions either. Studies estimate that 20 percent of World War II veterans suffered from PTSD. For veterans of Vietnam, the numbers were even higher, with an estimated 80 percent reporting that they still struggled with symptoms more than 20 years after the war. Some 20 percent of veterans from more recent wars are estimated to have PTSD symptoms, though some doctors believe the number to be higher. The reality of war is a brutal one, and its consequences are not only physical.

THOUGH PROVOKING
MOMENTS

In childhood, Louis was a troublemaker, but as he grew older, he realized what he was risking. During the 1930s, the Nazis weren't the only people interested in eugenics. When a boy in his town was declared mentally deficient and taken away to be forcibly sterilized, Louis realized that as an immigrant and a thief, he was a prime candidate for the eugenics agenda. He started trying to clean up his act.

This was not an isolated incident. Over the course of 54 years, California sterilized some 20,000 people. It's a moment over which to pause for thought. The Allies were certainly on the right side of the war, but they weren't perfect.

When Louis ran at Notre Dame, he was warned that coaches had told their players to sharpen the spikes on their shoes and slash him with them. Louis didn't believe this was something anyone would do, but he was later closed in by other runners, who stepped on his foot, cut open his shins, and elbowed him in the ribs. At the Olympics, Don Lash was boxed in by Finnish runners and elbowed in the stomach. Louis won his race. Lash did not.

Louis and Lash, in these cases, were a testament to sportsmanship. They did not fight back in the way they were fought against, but instead chose to do as much as they could within the bounds of honorable behavior. This in some ways foreshadows Louis' choice at the end of the book, when, after much struggle and anger, he forgives those who held him captive. He took the high road in the end, and it gave him peace.

As they rode toward Yokohama, former POWs cheered at the sight of bombed out Japanese cities, but the more they passed, the less jovial they were. They saw civilians who were starving, and realized the impact of the war on the Japanese people. At Naoetsu, the freed POWs had shared their food and supplies with the struggling natives.

War is difficult. It is hard on those who fight it away from home, and perhaps harder on those whose soil is the staging ground. In a society like that of Japan at the time, the people had very little say in the choices of the higher ups, and it was those same common people who suffered the most.

THOUGHTS FOR A SEQUEL

Lauren Hillenbrand was exceedingly thorough in her coverage of Louis' life from birth to death, following even the smallest details and even covering some of the lives and histories of those who came into contact with him. Because of this, there is not much room for a sequel focused on Louis, or even on Phil, as the most dramatic parts of his story overlap with Louis'. A possible sequel, instead, might explore the impact of Louis' legacy on others. As Hillenbrand's interest in Louis was first stirred by mention of him in many sources while doing research for her book on Seabiscuit, it is conceivable that she would already have research in this area.

CONCLUSION/FINAL ANALYSIS

It is little wonder that *Unbroken* drew such a large audience. Its story is exactly the kind many people enjoy most – the triumph of good over evil, and a journey from struggle and torment to freedom. For such a gripping story, however, and particularly one with such a heart wrenching subject *Unbroken* is perhaps somewhat lacking in emotional depth. Certainly, the stories of Louis' suffering are enough to stir emotion in readers, but much more is said of the physical conditions in which Louis' lived during his years in Japan than of his emotional state.

That is not to say the book is entirely without mention of Louis' emotions. There are moments in which they come through quite clearly. At other times, they are harder to gauge. Perhaps Hillenbrand simply didn't wish to speculate on any emotions Louis' didn't specifically mention himself.

There are moments of the story that stretch credibility. The story of Louis, Phil, and Mac's fight with the sharks which were jumping over the sides of the collapsing raft, for example, is hard to believe, and that Louis and other survived constant head injury with little to no brain damage is something of a miracle. However, it is often said that real life is stranger than fiction, and where a fiction writer would, in fact, have had to tone some of Louis' stories down to make suspension of disbelief possible, in a non-fiction book that is not necessarily the case.

Overall, the story is an enthralling one and Louis Zamperini, despite his early run as a thief and a troublemaker, is a character the reader can't help but pull for.

Made in the USA
Columbia, SC
19 August 2019